THE GRACE TO LEAVE

For Pam,
    So great to see
    you!!
    May the idiots
    in NY wake up...

with love,
    Lola
    12/6/2012

VAN K. BROCK
FLORIDA POETRY SERIES

ANHINGA PRESS

ALSO BY LOLA HASKINS

POETRY

Still, the Mountain
Silver Medal, Florida Book Awards, 2010
Paper Kite Press, 2010

Solutions Beginning with A
(illustrated by Maggie Taylor), Modernbook, Palo Alto CA, 2007

Desire Lines, New and Selected Poems
BOA Editions, 2004

The Rim Benders
Anhinga Press, 2001

Extranjera
Story Line Press, 1998

A Lifetime from Any Land We Knew
(chapbook) Yarrow, Kutztown University, 1998

Hunger
Edwin Ford Piper Award (Iowa Poetry Prize)
University of Iowa Press, 1993; second edition Story Line Press, 1996

Forty-Four Ambitions for the Piano
University Press of Florida, 1990; second edition Betony Press, 1994

Castings
Countryman Press, 1984; Second Edition, Betony Press, 1991

Across Her Broad Lap Something Wonderful
State Street Press, 1989

Planting the Children
University Press of Florida, 1983

PROSE

Fifteen Florida Cemeteries: Strange Tales Unearthed
University Press of Florida, 2011

Not Feathers Yet: A Beginner's Guide to the Poetic Life
Backwaters Press, 2007

Visions of Florida
Introductory essay to photographs by Woody Walters
University Press of Florida, 1994

THE GRACE TO LEAVE

POEMS

LOLA HASKINS

Lola Haskins

VAN K. BROCK
FLORIDA POETRY SERIES

ANHINGA PRESS

TALLAHASSEE, FLORIDA 2012

Cover art: "Car with Contrails," digital painting by Carol Lynne Knight
        based on a photo by Simon Beck
Cover design, book design, and production: Carol Lynne Knight
Type Styles: text and titles set in Adobe Minion Pro

Library of Congress Cataloging-in-Publication Data
The Grace to Leave by Lola Haskins, First Edition
ISBN – 978-1-934695-28-9
Library of Congress Cataloging Card Number – 2012933924

Anhinga Press Inc. is dedicated wholly to the
publication and appreciation of fine poetry and other literary genres.

For personal orders, catalogs and information write to:
Anhinga Press
P.O. Box 3665
Tallahassee, Florida 32315
Website: www.anhinga.org
Email: info@anhinga.org

Published in the United States
by Anhinga Press
Tallahassee, Florida
First Edition, 2012

For D'Arcy and Django

Contents

ACKNOWLEDGMENTS

88: "Green and Variations"

Adirondack Review: "What You Want"

Another Chicago Magazine: "For Those Who Will Not Vote"
and "Out of Order" as ("2005")

Atlantic Monthly: "The Ballad of Foot and Mouth"

Beloit Poetry Journal: "Sky Shots," "Perfection"

Crazyhorse: "Minnows," "Instructions from the Couturier"
and "The Return" (as "Walls")

Georgia Review: "Moor," "The Lake" (as "November 13, 2006"),
"The Considerations of My Teeth," "Moles," "Ode to the Otoliths,"
and "Some Geometries of Love"

Green Mountains Review: "To Prevail" (as "Story")
and "Parsing Mother"

In Posse: "Script for a French Movie"

Iris: "Hide and Seek"

Linebreak: "Belling"

Luna: "Performance Art"

Platte Valley Review: "The Sandhill Cranes" (as "The Grace to Leave")

Prairie Schooner: "Lascivion," "When Mother," "Brows," "Nostrils,"
and "Pavan for the Little Finger of the Right Hand"

Salamander: "The Good Host," "The Excavators," and "The Roman
Road from Skipton to Addingham"

Southern Review: "Daddy Who Can Say"

Tampa Review: "Will"

The God Particle: "The Sandhill Cranes"

"The Sandhill Cranes" was anthologized in *Snakebird:Thirty Years of Anhinga Poets* and *A Poets Guide to the Birds* (both Anhinga Press). In addition, it was included in a 2003 interactive CD produced by Steve Robitaille for the Florida Defenders of the Environment.

"What you Want" was featured on *Verse Daily.*

"Perfection" was featured on *Poetry Daily.*

"To Prevail" was included (as "Story") in *Northern Music, Poems Inspired by Glenn Gould,*" J.D. Smith, Ed., John Gordon Burke Publisher, 2001.

"Seven Turtles" appeared in *No War* (Utah State Poetry Society, 2002) and in *The Recycled Quarterly* as "November, 2001." It was also included in "Scattered Voices," music by James Paul Sain, and performed at the International Electroacoustic Music Composers Convention, 2003, and at the Society of Electroacoustic Composers Annual convention, 2004. In addition, it was reprinted as a broadside by Kelli Russell Agodon in a series of poems against the Iraq War.

Love and gratitude to my friends and partners in poetic crime: Fleda Brown, Sidney Wade, Brandon Kershner, Joe Haldeman, and Nicholas Samaras.

THE GRACE TO LEAVE

Seven Turtles

On the Withlachoochee last Saturday,
seven turtles in graduated sizes queued
on a log, routine as the osprey nests,
empty this time of year, normal as

the occasional alligator, its blunt nose
and hooded eyes half-submerged,
as are most fears most of the time,
until a plane slams into a building

or a son can't be found. We are
spoiled, you and I, guilty of
saying of the good dark bread
on our plates not *How delicious*

but *Where's the rest?* And so
with the turtles, the osprey nests,
even the palms leaning so low
they parallel the water. But now

a wood stork crosses our bow.
And another. And when we
look left, to where river-flow
complicates into cypress creek,

we see them: hundreds of wood storks
with their black-edged wings,
hunched like priests in the trees.
And I remember a morning

in Cairo, years ago, when the veiled
figure next to me, on the side of
the aisle that was all women,
turned, and took my western hands

in hers as if my fingers might
be breakable, as if she loved them,
and said, in the only language
we both understood: *Pass this on.*

1
BODY ENGLISH

Brows

Rain pours off the eaves The house of my eyes is safe

The painter kneels The gestures of wrist and brush live in the air

Here are the tracks some long ago traveler left over the dunes

Beyond them, the land stretches to where mist covers the mountains

I rest in calm awareness

The Considerations of My Teeth

My teeth nestle around the edges of their cave like campers waiting for a bonfire. They pass the time by telling stories involving old moths, or must, or chipotle. At night they work the gone day into powder.

My teeth wouldn't mind being piano keys, and sometimes they try to mimic the way an ocean arcs, but always in the end they fail, and fall back down to where the air surrounding them is dark pink as if the sun were about to come up or had just disappeared.

On the tops of some of my teeth are small hollows like beggars' cups but the indentations may be seen as tide pools or refuges instead and my teeth think about this. Sometimes they feel small-animal furry to themselves, sometimes slick as ice, and for those few moments they imagine they can let all this slide off ...

their prisoner lives, the years they will spend underground side by side, rocking in the jawbone. And it occurs to them as well, that one day they may find themselves lifted free and pierced, then strung to adorn the neck of a young woman like the one I once was, though they will have forgotten me in their long rest.

ODE FOR THE OTOLITHS

The doctor said there were stones in my ears and I did not believe her,
but you are. And when I bend my head you fall into the arms of cilia
that wave like undersea plants, for sound is what happens when we
reach the sandy depths toward which we have been descending
                                                        and close
our eyes as a piano streams its notes and Beethoven turns into tears.

The doctor said there were stones in my ears and I did not believe her,
but suddenly here you are, like the minute discoveries of an enthralled
two year old. There is so much of myself I have not met: caves and
tubes and labyrinths, named for Romans or scientists peering into
microscopes. But someone called you what you were: "ear stones,"
like a child given "John" who has been, in every life, simply "John."

The doctor said there were stones in my ears and I did not believe her.
Until the day you lodged. First jumping on one foot failed me then
dancing, however wild, then all the doctor's instruments. I staggered
and clutched to keep from falling. Oh my daughter, never — as you
look into my face that loves you, into your garden, into the night
                                            above your house —
imagine anything will be always there. Not me, not flowers, not stars.

NOSTRILS

When I was a horse, they were velvety oblongs and I galloped
over blue-eyed grass. When I was a dog, they were taupe
and moist, and could make out even mouselings, deep
inside their holes. When I was a young man, son of a Lord,
they filled with stone damp. When I married, they
smelt instead peacock and partridge, roasting in an oven
wider and taller than I. When I was a little girl I used to flare
them wide. I would dream I ran over the plains. I thought
long silken whinny were the most beautiful words in the world.

Pavan for the Little Finger of the Right Hand

You told me you don't matter, as you helped wipe my white plates dry.
But listen:

Without you, how could Debussy have owned the C
that soared like an angled wing?

Without you, anything hurled would lose its way.

Without you, my cheek would be missing its fifth touch.

And if you were gone, little sister, how I would mourn your nail,
of all the rest most like a shell.

And how the dishtowel loves the edge where you meet the air.
You are all the world to it: a shore, a hill.

KNUCKLES

The Master taught me to fold my fingers, cock my arm then push it straight, first right, then left. I would *ke-yi* with each impact, legs bent, back rigid. When the sky darkened and lightning began to strike the field, the Master told me stay. I did not question him but punched the flashing night while rain coursed down the cliffs of my knuckles and my hair streamed black over my eyes. Tell me Master, Sensei of my Heart, you who died last year at the bottom of your garden. Shall I stop?

Moles

Constellations   Archipelagos   The heads of swimming animals

Umlauts   Ellipses   Dust on a tabletop   Speckles on a shell

Time leaves its mark so quietly I hardly noticed

until this morning   There, above my lip

CAPILLARIES

I love how they are so narrow even a kayak couldn't turn, trapped at a bend between tidal grasses, flattened where an alligator may have slept at noon. I love how they rise and fall with the pull of my breath, how they carry messages like tubes in banks, swishing up and out of sight.

I love that my body has many tributaries like these, fine as hairs lit by oxygen. I love that these tiny rivers never position themselves in front of me saying, *Don't you get it? I need, I need.* I love that without my participation, a bright red cardinal hopped onto the feeder this morning and fed a white seed to its ruffly adolescent's open beak.

There are so many reasons to be happy in this world.

ODE TO MY SMALL HAIR

In the beginning you were as sparse
as walkers on a winter beach. Then
you deepened, not to a cove but
to the dark hills that rise beside it.

Keep me safe from the wind, here
where my small boat lulls, until
the one who finds his way to me
lights these waters until they glow.

Of the True Ankle Joint

i

How else can I say it?
Every step I take I owe.

ii

The triumvirate,
femur, fibula, and talus,
orders the metatarsals on.

Before their advancing ranks, the phalanges
lay down their tributes of white pearls.

iii

Consider love, consider fine china:
One hairline, almost invisible, fracture,
and the tea will seep unstoppably into your hand.

The Great Toe

The great toe is a house with one window.

The great toe's son is taller than she   yet tender to her mind.

Seen from the ocean   the great toe is a tower rimed with salt.

A pale line crosses the great toe   as of something flown.

A moment leaves the world that way   one streak

across the sky   then gone.

Footsoles

resemble sand whorled by the tide around an inlet   the arch

～

live on the ground floors of leather houses

～

have thickened under their loads

～

distorted for vanity's sake turn on themselves ashamed

～

wake sometimes fearing that   weighing nothing   they do not exist

The Roman Road from Skipton to Addingham

I used to be young. Now, I pick my way from broken stone to broken stone. Below me lie fields, and in the blurred distance where the fields end, other moors. I feel safe here, flanked as I am by low blueberries and harebells and dock gone to reddish seed. But suddenly the air explodes, as from both sides the legions of gorse close in. Where are my chariots now? The answer is only the silence of this bright afternoon, and the clouds that still swim in the standing water. How casually they let the centuries fall.

The Ballad of Foot and Mouth

One-ery, Two-ery, Ziccary, Zeven
Hollow-bone, Crack-a-bone, Ten-or-eleven
Spin, Spun, It-must-be-done

So they push them up— the ewes,
the wethers, the lambs, the tupps—
With their yellow dozers like flowers o

Eena, Deena, Dina, Dust
Catt'lla, Jweena, Wina, Wust

With their yellow dozers like flowers o
The wethers, the half-grown lambs, the tupps
in mountains now with their legs stiff up

Ein, Tein, Tethra, Methera, Pimp
Awfus, Daufus, Deefus, Dumfus, Dix

In mountains now with their legs stiff up
The wethers, the half-grown lambs, the ewes
And what is motherhood now o

One-ery, Two-ery, Ziccary, Zeven
Hollow-bone, Crack-a-bone, Ten-or-Eleven
Spin, Spun, It-must-be-done

And what is motherhood now o
as the ash smoulders in the backs of our throats
of the ewes, the wethers, the half-grown lambs

And the moors all empty but for the wind
that moans as it licks at the dry stone walls
And that's your motherhood now o

Spin, Spun, It-must-be-done
Twiddledum, Twaddledum, Twenty-one.

Note: In 2001, the English government responded to a foot and mouth epidemic by preventively incinerating thousands and thousands of sheep. When they were reintroduced, the heafing instinct by which sheep know to graze towards the fields in which they were born, had to start over, presenting a major problem for North Yorkshire farmers, especially those with open moorland.

Moor

1

And what survives? Only the voracious:
gorse with its dark green prickles,
its seeds that pop like a greedy baby's lips;
bracken whose spores in fall cause cancer;
heather, tough, clumping in gangs
that turn bruised in August — tiny purple blossoms that blend
with distance as if a thumb had smudged the page.
And each of these tries to choke the rest.
I am the only one, says the heather, the gorse.
I will kill you if I can, says the bracken.

Or, nothing grows but the barest grass, stretched to near
transparency,
like the features of a dancer over bone.

There are no cattle here, with their soft eyes.
Only the primitive-headed, the slope-muzzled, their blatting
the sound of words before there was language:
Herdwicks and Jacobs and Lonks,
bred to heaf to their home-grounds if they stray too far.
Summers, wind blows hard over the moor.
In winter, snow frenzies and swirls until all track's lost,
like a crofter who clenches a fist at his door,
as something he does not understand pours from
his mouth. When the snow stops, the farmers go
prospecting, prod at the drifts with sticks.
Once, Moon dug out eight ewes and a wether.
The storm had lasted ten days.
One had died, but the rest had eaten each other's wool.

What can dig, does. You can walk for hours and see only evidence:
the dark clustered droppings like full-stops gone wild. But then
the sudden ground will crawl—as tens of brown scuts zigzag
into heather or between rocks. More often, you stumble
over them first, scribbles of fur and bone—blinded, starved.

2

Fresh from Australia, Megan went hiking, the ordnance survey
for Yorkshire, West (her uncle's) in its see-through case
on a cord around her neck,
the way little girls have their names pinned
to their first-day-of school dresses
thought Megan, who'd done the outback, the Rockies, and, last year,
Nepal, but said only: *I'll call you when I get to Grassington*
before she set out,
cigarette dangling from one red-nailed hand, along paths never more
than ten miles, she knew, from a pub.
But the moor can change, like a woman with a knife
in her handbag who makes eyes across the room.
And no map, no piece of paper at all, no page from
the psalms, no verse from the Quran, not even James Joyce
can hold back the mist.
And the moor turned suddenly white.
And four times Megan stopped.
And four times she'd have stepped off a cliff.

3

A moor's a wrong turn a blank wall
days spent staring
when I've been nowhere
for months
But I come back again and again
I can't stay gone
Because once
the mist lifted and I realized
why I was out of breath

I was at the top —
and from this top I could see other tops
purple, dark green, dark brown
and the far profiles of old women —
mountains in the distance —
and in that moment I understood
what three hundred sixty degrees meant
to my soul

and I believed I could climb
the other peaks as well
though there were valleys between
with their cities glittering like grass
and their smug Wednesday church bells
though there were A-roads between
with their worms of smoke
though there were walled pastures between
where brown-and-whites grazed,
false maps on their sides

And in that moment this was my religion:
if only
I could keep courage in my knees
the days of walking, with nothing to show but miles
the long afternoons of up
the slash-eyed wind
the rocks to navigate by rain
the mud
even the redux mist
even the unstarred night
would not matter

And when breath came hard
as breath does I would know

I was not dying
but ascending another scale,
like the curlew for whom flight is not
enough   but she must sing too.

Note: Because the footpath system in Britain is so old, many of
the paths are unclear, so serious hikers carry Ordnance Survey
maps, small-scaled grid-reference charts that show altitude
changes as well as footpath routes. They include details like walls,
stiles, buildings, and farm roads too small to be included on other
maps. These maps are usually opened to the relevant area, and
hung in plastic cases around the hiker's neck. This is partly to
keep them dry and partly so the hiker can walk, hands-free and
find his/her way without digging into a backpack.

The Return

We used to live here, the woman says,
taking the boy's hand.
I don't remember, says the boy.
Were there sheep here then?

Oh yes, says his mother. They used
to bump into our bedroom wall at night.
We thought they were visitors
at first, but when we looked

outside, there were only sheep.
Were we living in a house?
asks the boy. Of course, says
his mother. And she picks up

a thick ceramic arrowhead.
And we ate off these.
When they were plates,
she adds. And we used to sit

on our front steps, and drink tea.
See those bumpy lines of rock
across the beck? Those are
bronze-age fields, and once

we slid down them on a tray.
That was the morning
the sun turned the snow
almost blue. Remember?

They have walked steep slopes
to get here. The boy spreads
his arms. His mother
picks him up, cradles

his head against her
shoulder, and soon he's
limp. She considers
the rubble at her feet

now she's alone, but it's
as speechless as the heap of
stones in the field above, that's
Bombey's Barn on the map.

Who was Bombey? She
doesn't know. And who was
she, baby on hip, trudging
happily along this path,

muddy no matter what the weather?
Who was she when her hair smelt
of kerosene? She looks across
the beck, and senses as if it were

her own pulse against her palm,
the curled damp of her boy's hair.
And slowly the long days return
when what mattered was stones,

rough, pitted, the biggest
she could find. And she leans

backwards, lugs them up-slope
to the half-made wall,

and drops them one by one
like heavy mice, at the feet of
the squat man she loves. And
the boy murmurs in his sleep,

When you were speckled, Mom,
when we lived on the cliff,
before there were walls,
when we used to be a bird.

2

THE LAKE

What You Want

When the rough-faced sea ignites the western clouds
and the horizon disappears When black pitching

grabs your heart and the hatch leaks   When it comes
to you how high your mast is and how it desires lightning

When you drop the main and cling to the slick deck,
your lifeline sliding along the rail so you slip

and splay and are less than man   When the woman you love
is safe on land and the son and the daughter can't help

When all this convenes, a salt calm enters your soul
where great fish cruise above the coral, and anemones

extend their hunting fingers And in a beat you understand
that it was never her gleaming surface that sirened you

from the marina, with its safe posts and pretty flags,
but rather what lies underneath, that it's she you crave

more deeply than your life, she who is made of sand
and darkness, she who will never abandon you.

Belling

The owls' sobs overlap, as if the beginning of weeping
were so profound
as to call its sister from across the trees.
In our rumpled bed, we lie listening. You remember the grandfather
who made you kites and how,
when he died, you lost your only parent.
I think of how easily
I've betrayed you, over and again for poetry.
Sheets of moonlight fall across us.
In a city thousands of miles from here, a woman
is overcome by the shining bay.
She hunches, her head in her wet hands.

The Hawk

Every afternoon as I slide around the sandy curve, he sails across my bow, beautiful as an evening purse, each wing perfectly speckled, each dip and rise an arc I could spend a life naming.

He lives in the tangled depths of sweet gum and magnolia and flies always to the field where live oaks spread their branches to the grass. And always now, to spiral into the violet air. And lately I have become aware of my bald self, how it beats as it scuttles for its burrow. What is the meaning of your claws at the edge of my sight, my love? What is this circling?

Two Dreams and a Luminary

1 Script for a French Movie

When they open his head, there's nothing inside. *But it's so white*, says his wife, looking around. The surgeon's mask indents damply, and his eyes have no dots in them and she sees that he is a cartoon.

Only a cartoon, she tells herself, as she flips the pages of *Elle*. And yet ... When a cartoon caresses another cartoon, then goes home and tells his wife he is leaving her and means it and then not, and means it and then not, does she not cry?   Night after night, does she not cry?   And if a cartoon beats his wife, will her bones not break?   And are not her teardrops grief?

When she visits his room the next morning, her husband's bandaged skull looks like an egg. She sees that everything has been boiled out of him. *No Wonder!* appears in the bubble over her head. She stands beside his bed and holds the limp fish of his hand. Slowly, the bubble empties and floats gone.

2. Lascivion

Leaning on a rail overlooking
the sea, he thinks to commit crimes
in my hair. And will. And the law?
Leave that to judges and dry readers.
Here everything flows:
froth to shore, the stranded kelp
that stays wet for days, the steam
that will not stop rising.

3. To Prevail

It was the New York Philharmonic, Bernstein conducting. Glenn Gould was the soloist. The subject was Brahms. And, with a small group attending, it was the one rehearsal. Gould began the first movement with such languidity that the orchestra was disappearing over the horizon as Bernstein waved it to a stop. This is not our tempo, Bernstein said. And, more to the point, this is not what Brahms wanted. But Gould said: *I am Canadian. And I know something about mountains. And I know something about genius, which is like a mountain. And I know how this piece should be played, which is like the snow that lies quiet and glittering on the Rockies.* And Gould was cold in this, and adamant as diamonds.

The next evening, Bernstein bowed, shook his head until his hair was wild, and announced to the darkened seats: *As the soloist and I cannot agree, I have decided to accompany him. But I want you to know I hate this, with all the fury that sends snow suddenly down mountains to bury young men with their illusions of immortality.* Then he turned to the orchestra and he raised his baton.

HIDE AND SEEK

I am only considered hiding if someone may be seeking. This is the heart of what I am doing behind this shut door under striped sheets, and in my hands Alane's pink and green book pouring out, with all the sorrow of too many flowers, the difficulty of any intimate love, of a statue which puts a stone hand on the right breast of another statue and is thereby joined to her forever. And I can hear you looking for me or rather I can hear the boards creak under your shoes and I can hear the living room door stick, defying closure the way a teenager, sulky, obeys and does not obey.

Now you're sending music after me, love songs whose words you know I know, and I'm fighting to hear Alane as the songs penetrate the glass and wood between us. They roll me under and force salt water down my throat and sand against my teeth and I'm holding my breath hard. When I surface I still have the book in my hands but it's waterlogged as if by tears.

I read the first line of something. The doorknob turns and you come into my room, wanting to lift away without touching, any cloth which lies between you and my skin. And that is what I wish too, deeper than the light that lies in rubies, and it is also what I abhor, with the same force in my soul that wants the sea to dry and the sun to turn cold then colder, until the world sinks into jagged glitter and we feel nothing at all.

Tin Roof

The drops thicken, then ravish down.
And in the suddenly-close room
as her husband's mouth bubbles on,
she realizes that flocks of storms are
still migrating, that it is not too late.

At the creek one morning, a green needle
linking four black wings shows her
as clearly as if it wrote on air
how to stay here for the rest of her life.
If only we could live always on the verge

of shivering, on the cliff-edge of too much,
breath stopped upon a table. Yet I think
what we must love instead is zero, that sky
where sounds collide and cancel. The night
the stranger pressed his jumpy gun against

my skull, all the words I could conjure
rushed out at once, to crisscross the dark
like bats. After awhile though, their
squeakings turned silent, sweet as a box
to crawl into: a spaceship, a house, a train.

The Good Host

When the guest you didn't invite arrives, you don't take his coat
to put on the bed with the others or offer him a drink or lead him
to the group by the fire. Instead, you try to shut the door in his face.

But then he presents his invitation, with its two tiny hand-prints
and you realize you've asked him after all, though when
you planned your party it was not he you had in mind

but rather a friend who sips your wine, deep red as a heart,
and smiles at you gently. Regiments of glasses stand in waves,
like rows of crosses the sun has loved. They slow you

just enough, that when the bell rings again, it is the guest
who strides across the room, to return with bodies, wilted
over his arms to lay out *hush now* on the darkened bed.

Sky Shots

Magic Trick

Someone is working late in the sky's tall buildings. Bent nearly double, he has shredded the flames that are floating down now.

~

Constellations

I could not drive between the sky's towns if I had more spangles than a glacier.

~

White

We are standing in the palazzo of a minor prince whose caretaker has thrown sheets over all the furniture.

~

Moon

The mother has scissored a black circle for her child to glue.

~

*

See the bottom of the page.

~

Startled

The air bangs. That leggy flash is you, entering the ground.

~

Upside-Down Bowl

If you live in a tea-garden, yours will be the size of a cup.
If a prairie, only sun, dripping off the edges, can show you
where it ends.

— *In memoriam, Reetika Vazirani*

The Lake

November 13, 2006

It's my birth day and the men in the waiting room are passing out cigars, it's a girl they're saying, and I am, and my father was not there because he was on what I learned when I was two was a destroyer on a faraway ocean whose name I was not ready to pronounce.

It's my birth day and on the curved shore of an island an alligator is gathering the warmth that keeps what she has eaten from rotting, and killing her from the inside. As I pass, she bellies into the red-brown water and becomes a log.

It's my birth day. I'm walking single around Alice, with her leaning moss-draped oaks and her cypresses, and her moorhens scattered like kanji among the reeds, and her shadows so close to the sky they have almost disappeared yet in an instant can dive and rise, silver in their claws.

If I pluck the highest string of the instrument I carry, might I hear the overtones of what 60,000 bats are dreaming in their darkened city across the road, the bats that will turn the dusk as heavy as the perfume of a woman who wants so much she can scarcely breathe? She waits, she waits, she thinks them gone, then flutters break the dim as winged mice faster and faster dip over her hair, then circle and dive over the lake like handkerchiefs, so hungry they are.

3

Some Geometries of Love

Anguish as a Second Language

Of what is your hometown made? Wood? Concrete? Mud?
How easily do its buildings burn or push over? How do you know?

Write in your grandfather's voice, beginning at dusk on a summer day.

Tell us about an uncle you loved as a child. Where is he now?

Tell how it is different here, waking up at night.

You are a window. Describe the street outside.

How do you say "happy" and "sad" in your language? Translate.

SOME GEOMETRIES OF LOVE

Triangle

One afternoon, we shrugged on backpacks and set out over Rombald's Moor. After a few miles, we cut across a field. The rain had stopped, leaving a quiet so profound we could hear tufts of grass being ripped, as sheep twisted them off their roots. Finally, we crested a hill. When we tried to climb the wall on the other side, we dislodged it instead, because the stones lay together under an agreement to which we were not parties. And that night under the bedclothes, something woke me, and I knew that whatever I'd sworn, I did not love you, but loved only the part of my foot beneath the second toe that was green and purple — I could feel it — and throbbing in the dark.

Circle

How many ways can six pigs look at each other if each pig looks at one other pig and each pig is looked at by at least one pig? It is problems like this that cause so many poets to abandon paper and pencil after high school. It's not that they can't compute. It's that the possibilities frighten them. And also because they understand that even if they did derive the very answer listed upside down on page 69, it would be beside the point since in philosophy every proposition is, in the end, unknowable. For instance: although Jason may look at Margaret and be seen by Joe, and John may look at Jenny and be seen by Sue, what happens if Joe has only one leg or John is deaf? And what is the effect of Erin's Catholicism? To answer such questions, there are not enough pencils in the world.

Pentagon

The shortest distances between Father, Mother, Son, Daughter, and
Daughter describe a building solidified in its field by the way the Mother
need only look at her Son, for him to say, *Mother, I know*; and the way
the Mother and the Daughters sit in restaurant booths for hours after
the food is gone; and the way the Father and the big Daughter adore
hardware stores together; and the way the Father writes, asking his
Son's advice because the Father does not know how to look up Peace in
his Chinese dictionary but the Son can tell him the radicals instantly.
Such a building is very strong. But pregnable nevertheless, to a pilot
whose greatest desire is to die. And so, penetrated, five shrinks to four;
and an arm, half a leg, and a shoe. There is a pause, during which the
sky becomes small. Finally, the four look up from their laps, and decide
to start again. But yard after builder's yard is strewn with dust. There is
no brick anywhere, in all that wide town.

THE EXCAVATORS

Lift the bones gently, held together by their clothes, while groups of burkaed women watch, as if what they could see again might be their sons not these jackknifed heaps.

Lay their burdens out in rows until the dead stretch over the sloping hills, who would have thought the earth to have borne so many, an exercise in perspective for the cross-legged god with the pad in his lap.

Turn aside periodically, to splash something bitter to the ruffed dirt like a map of a marsh or a group of dim and jagged figures, staggering forward.

Dig from red sun to red sun as fleas dot their legs; crouch to brush away the final dirt as the black-cloaked flocks crowd closer; do not, ever, look inside their skins at what they lift now.

For Those Who Will Not Vote

Election Eve, 2004

Clouds like great ships cross the predawn sky.
While you sleep, dark figures are securing the city.

Enlightenment

As the heron lifts it free,
the fish suddenly
understands.

A Partial Roll Call

— May 2004

Zach, Kyle, Matt
Ken, Thom, Rob
Brett, Ken, Nat

Kerman, Aaron, Jason
Kirk, Dean, Bill
Ryan, Tim, LaMont

Walter, William, David
Brian, Pat, Sahib
Jakub, Andrew, Bala

Dominic, Doug, José
Richard, Justin, Marlin
Henry, Cedric, Hans

Jesus Jesus

Out of Order

The lords of the year come up the river
in their stately boat. If the sun comes out,

their suited minions move the air. If it rains,
an arched roof is lifted over their heads.

The lords of the year come up the river
in their stately boat. Despite the blood

pooling in the streets like oil. Despite
the villagers whose huts have been

sentenced to rubble, so are loading
everything they own on carts.

The lords of the year come up the river
waving like homecoming queens.

Where is the assassin in his aerie?
Where is the swimmer in the dark water?

4

The Grace to Leave

Two Years on: Instructions from the Couturier

Pull up the dress of the waters. How clear it is, how small bright fish swim across your chest. Now let the day dim to green then rose. Let the sun slide into the slot behind the horizon. Let the jackpot dark come on with its millions of stars, huge bowls of them emptying over your upturned face.

Wear in your ears the evening song of the wren. From now on, as you tilt your head left and right before the mirror, there will flourish these tiny shinings. Notice how the wren's bourée enters — the hammer and anvil and stirrup arranged on each side, like girls at a dance, to take it in.

Decorate your shoulders with the bream in the pond. You've been promoted to a rank you could not have imagined in a military to which you did not know you belonged. Soon you will be striding out to sweep the unhappy, like fallen leaves, into piles, to say, fish flapping at your shoulders, *just look at yourselves, red and orange and yellow, like fires without a match, just look!*

GREEN AND VARIATIONS

The young satsuma leaves believe they will love their twigs
forever, will never harden into them like old women
in bitter dresses.

Look at us, the wild garlics purr,
See the latest from the ditches...
as they twitch their slender hips in the wind.

The smilax emerges straight, with a tender mane.
As he grows, he will turn feral and gallop
between the trees.

The sweetgums are waving their hands in the air
like kindergarteners.
Teacher Spring leans forward. They are
all in love with her.

They dream she smooths their branches as if
they were bedclothes, those long, rustling
evenings after school.

I am Five

There are so many birds
Mummy. Sometimes the sky
feels busier than school.
Why do I never find them dead?

Do dead birds turn into leaves?
Is it their bones I crunch under
my saddle shoes? Oh Mummy,
I think I am afraid of trees.

Minnows

The squared shade of water under the dock is the most elaborate brooch that ever quivered silver. The open pond is its dress, floor-length and flowing after the rain. And now through its long folds sun touches skin, the sand of which we are made, under which who can say what we may be thinking: *We are young? We will not be young again?* The pond has as many names as the boy gives the constellations, which surge in great arcs over his head, long after his parents have bowed deeply, each to each, and left the floor.

Daddy, Who is to Say You Have Flown Too Far

You can't be seen any more behind the moon's
extravaganza. You're someplace they haven't
named yet but I think it does have a name, maybe
Dark Sky Mountain, the one you started climbing
when you rose and your body became wrinkles
and weighed less by the heft of your soul.

When I was a child I left churches forever
because I thought they might blow down
and because I didn't trust their priests,
who knew only to talk and talk as if
the heat from their mouths would brand
belief on my skin like so many roses.

I think you're past the tree line on that mountain
by now Daddy, and onto balding ground which is
more beautiful than anything you could have told me,
holding me on your lap one of those rare evenings
you were home. Though I remember your singing
Blue Sky Day, early, when your chest hairs would
glitter as if it had rained during the night. And
mornings on the way to school when I'd watch
your lips in the rear view mirror and make mine

the same. They came in their hundreds in the end —
to mourn you, yes, but also to see if you might have left
any of your tongue behind. And when they saw you had,
they folded the paper very small, and put it in the pockets
of their suits. I am holding to you now Daddy, writing
your poems when you were younger than my son and bent
over your leather-bound book which asked only the highest
of you, and I think of the pilot your friend, who fell in flames
over Germany, and how gorgeously you sent him down.

Parsing Mother

You drop your camouflage one cloud at a time, until only cobalt unmercy remains.

You're rusty-green as dock on the verges, half-poison so I have to boil you three times and pour the waters away. But, you know, I get these cravings when I remember falsely how you held me and crooned me to sleep at night. And I can't help going back, bending over to fill my hands with what makes them burn.

You're a bird for the book I keep in the kitchen in case an unknown hammers at the window. I try to match your feathers, the cut of your beak. I look up the way you fly.

You're the dirt you crammed into my mouth with both hands. I root myself in you. Or the water that stands in ditches after rain, dark brown and without life.

You're the twig that slashed my eye as I pushed through branches. Why I see cracks, faults, flaws, in every vase and daughter. O Mother how declensions abound: nominative sun, accusative moon.

PERFORMANCE ART

Mother's monogrammed towels reek of smoke when we three go to clean out her apartment. It's raining. Rain's an anagram for what took Mother's mustache off. Before that, I used to find her straight black hairs stuck at angles in caramel wax, in the turquoise frying pan she kept in a bathroom drawer. We divide the rings, the carpets, the African lamps.

Finally, there is only Mother. I hang her in a quilted bag with the other clothes I never wear. Daddy is my wardrobe. I take bits of him and pin them all over my body. I will paint out my eyes, sit among sharp rocks for hours, in Korea, under the winter sun.

PERFECTION

The chameleon on the window vanished
without seeming to move. So am I
looking through the chameleon now,
as I gaze across the pasture?

Nana

Each drop of sea contains
all the fish that have ever lived,
each grit of sand the heart of
all the rocks that have risen
above the land or laid upon it.

When Ava, who is ten days old today,
cries, and I sing her the lullaby
that makes her head go soft against
my shoulder, she is every old woman
who has ever fallen asleep.

AT TWENTY-TWO MONTHS,
AVA LAUNCHES HER POETRY CAREER

Last month, you pointed at the dangling Christmas colors.
Stalactites! you said.

Last week, your Daddy held you upside down.
I don't like that, you said.

You don't like it? *No. I'm not a **bat**.*

Last night in the bath, you pressed three damp letters
to the tub wall.
C-A-T, you said. *Cat!*

When I asked you to spell dog, you put up: DGH
then said *Oh, I forgot the O!*
and added it: ODGH.   There's still hope.

Ava's Pony

You'd asked your mother what a range was and she'd said fields like
>ours, only bigger.

And you knew that horses lived on the range

and you wanted a horse more than you'd ever wanted anything

in all your six years, so you walked the woods and fences

with carrots in your pocket and your hand out, calling

>"Here Pony Pony."

Now if you thought when you came back alone it meant there was
>no pony,

it's my job to tell you what your mother didn't:

that dappled oak-light may turn into a pony at any moment,

that ponies may have been trotting through the sweet gums

just before you came. And remember that crackle of leaves

we heard on the other side of the creek?

If those could be deer, then why not ponies?

Let's go out again. See those tracks mingled with yours?

That must be where the ponies came.

I'll bet you didn't know they were looking for you.

Lydia and the Cicadas

Barefoot in her sister's dress
she picks their husks off
pine trunks, and lays them
carefully on her palm.
When it brims, she shakes
them into a jar which
she holds against the light
and studies, turning it
this way and that. What
has escaped her — she is three —
shelters in the humming grass.

Ode for Ava and Lydia

May you always be parading through your house
in your new dollar store underpants
carrying your new dollar store umbrellas.
May you be perpetually scooping dirt from your sandbox shovels
into the gaps around burlapped roses.

May you be teacher and student forever, you Ava,
doing downward dog with the full intensity of five,
you Lydia, losing your balance because your chubby legs
have had only two years to practice.

And may you, Ava, spell "looked" l-o-o-c-t for the rest of your life
and never lose the ear that finished "Cinderella" with a "u"
in your story where she finds a p-o-n-e and,
living happily ever after, rides it.

May neither of you forget how to follow the wavy crayon lines
you invented, at the ends of which
flocks of birds startle from the wild plums.

May you never be higher to the ground than you are now,
for without you, who will admire the tiny yellow flowers
on the heads of grass?

May you love me infinity plus infinity, and if that fails,
then more than all of outer space.
And when my Saturday car breaches the curve of your hill,
may you be watching at the window, then be
my two little suns forever, running out your door.

WILL

for D'Arcy and Django

My breath, mysterious to me
The long weathers of my arms
My eyes flecked like broken leaves
The crook of my elbow The secret
field under the curve of my hair:

All to be divided between you
so that when you who came from
my body start down our road
when the air is heavy and the frogs
are singing from the swamp
because it has rained or is about
to rain, I will be there.

But in the end — and you cannot
help this, every generation does
the same — you will drive me out.

I will be a rustle in the trees then
as if something had just flown. I
will be the skin that stills the standing
water. And when dusk falls, I will be
a single firefly, blinking green. For I can
never stop being amazed at your beauty,
my music-limbed boy, my woman who
loves numbers in her soul. But wait.
My love for you is hundreds of lanterns
searching the dark. In the gathering night,
look around. I will be *all* the fireflies.

The Sandhill Cranes

The blue air fills with cries.
The cranes are streams, rivers.
They danced on the night prairie,
leapt at each other, quivering.

The long bones of sandhill cranes
know their next pond. Not us.
When something is too beautiful,
we do not have the grace to leave.

About the Author

Lola Haskins taught Computer Science at the University of Florida for many years, and is currently (since 2006) on the faculty of Rainier Writers Workshop, a low residency MFA program at Pacific Lutheran University in Tacoma, Washington. She is the owner of a split heart, being passionate about both Florida and North Yorkshire. Most of the time, she lives in Gainesville, Fl.